Botanical Expressions
A Calming Escape

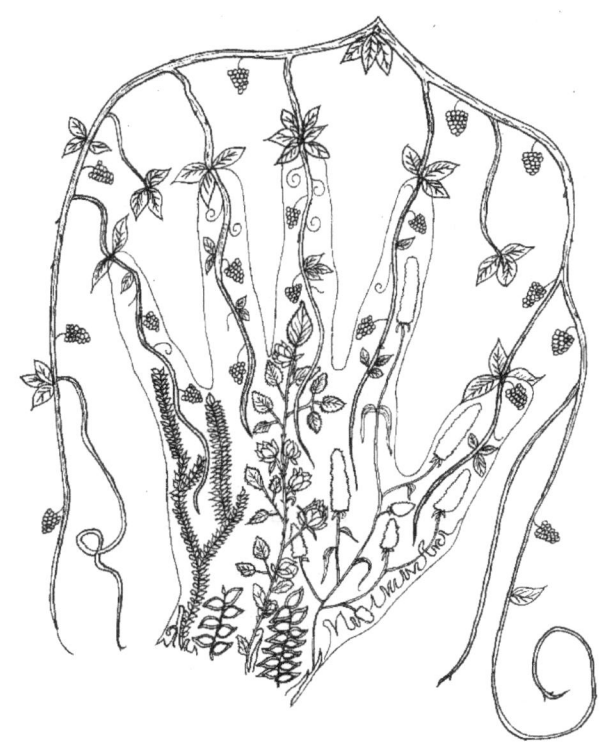

By Lei Faircloth

Copyright

Copyright © Lei Faircloth 2017

All rights reserved.

Bibliographical Note

Botanical Expressions is an original work, in a series of adult coloring books

created by

Lei Faircloth, in 2017.

ISBN-13: 978-1978419803

Botanical Expressions welcomes you!

Unleash your creativity adding color to over 20 hand-drawn designs created with care and love, for you to bring to life; you'll be inspired (and impressed) by your creativity.

This issue includes fun, imaginative, unique designs created on one page, which makes it easier for you to color using various coloring tools.

Some of the drawings feature my unique palm designs adorned with lovely flowers, vines, and whimsical trees. Each design differs in level of difficulty, so you can choose one that best fits your mood. (Who says you have to start on the first page!)

Have fun, and be sure to check out my upcoming coloring books in this series!

Sincerely,

Lei

Tester Page for your coloring tools!

Test your strokes, thickness of pencil points, and

intensity of markers and pens on this page.

Coloring tips:

* Use a blank sheet of paper/card under the page you are working on to prevent indentation or bleed-through on the next page.

* For intricate drawings, use fine tip markers, or well sharpened colored pencils for more precise filling in.

* Listening to classical music, or any music that relaxes you while working on this book can be therapeutic! I recommend YouTube® playlists featuring composers like, Chopin (Complete Nocturnes), Bach, Erik Satie, or soothing Adagios from various composers.

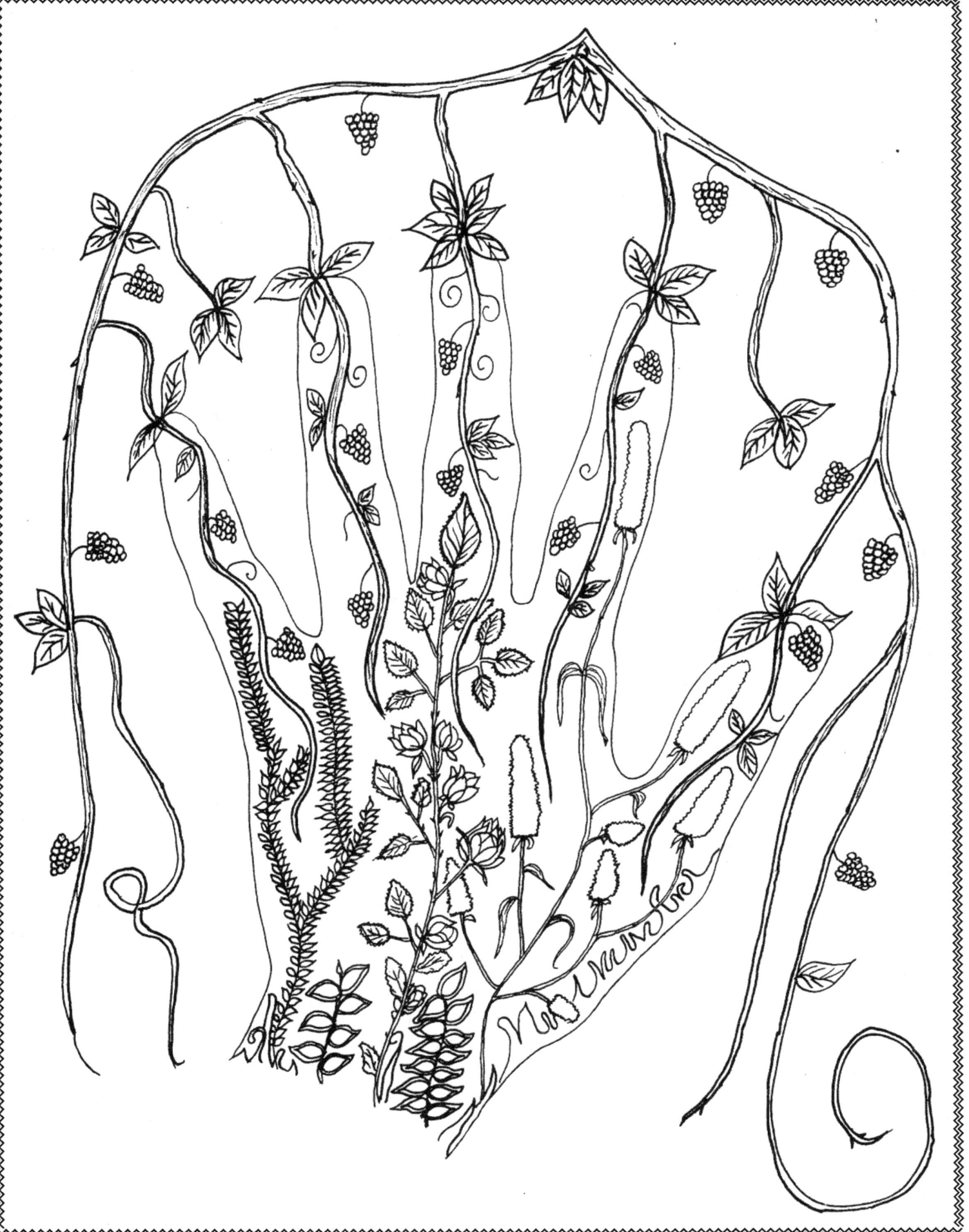

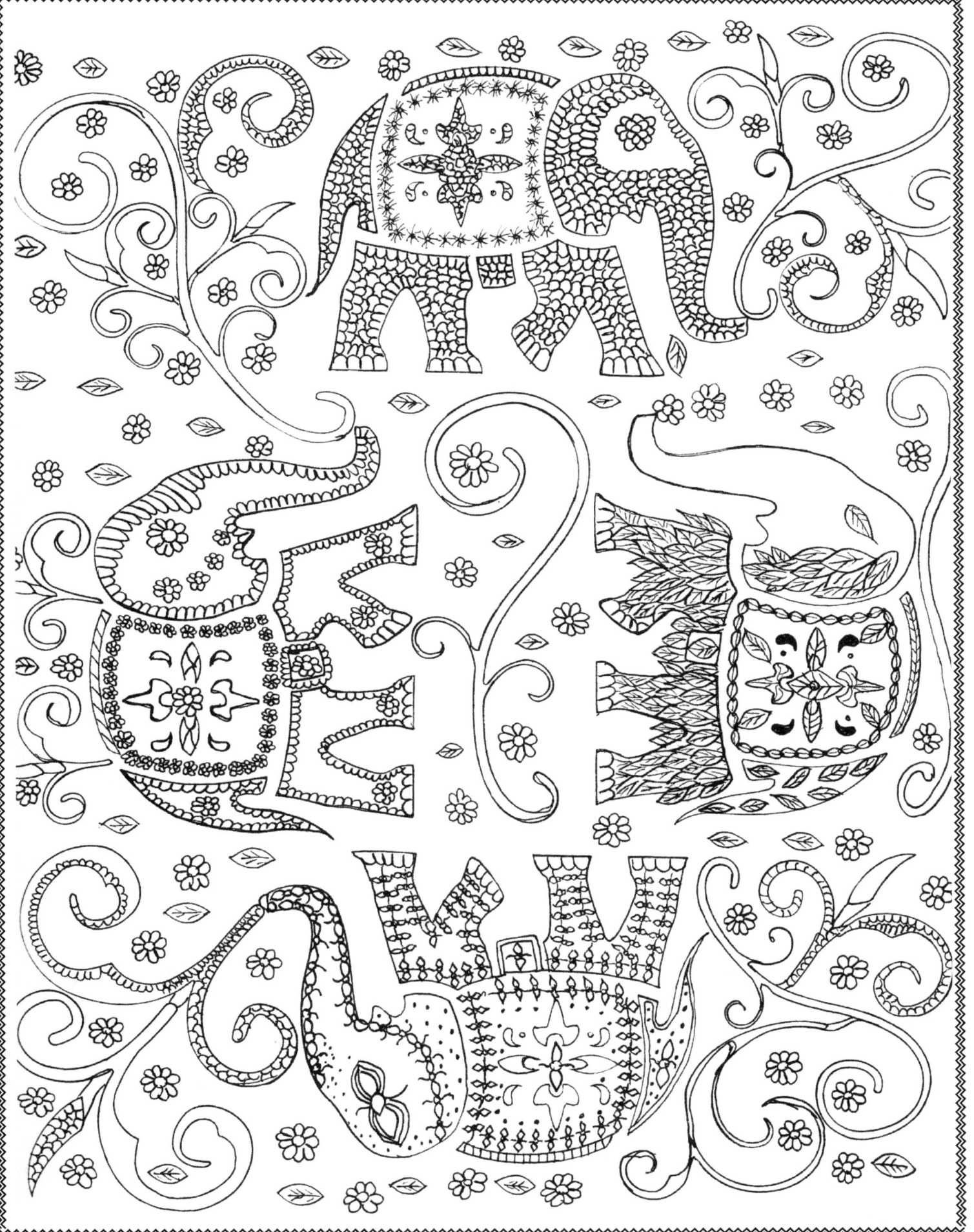

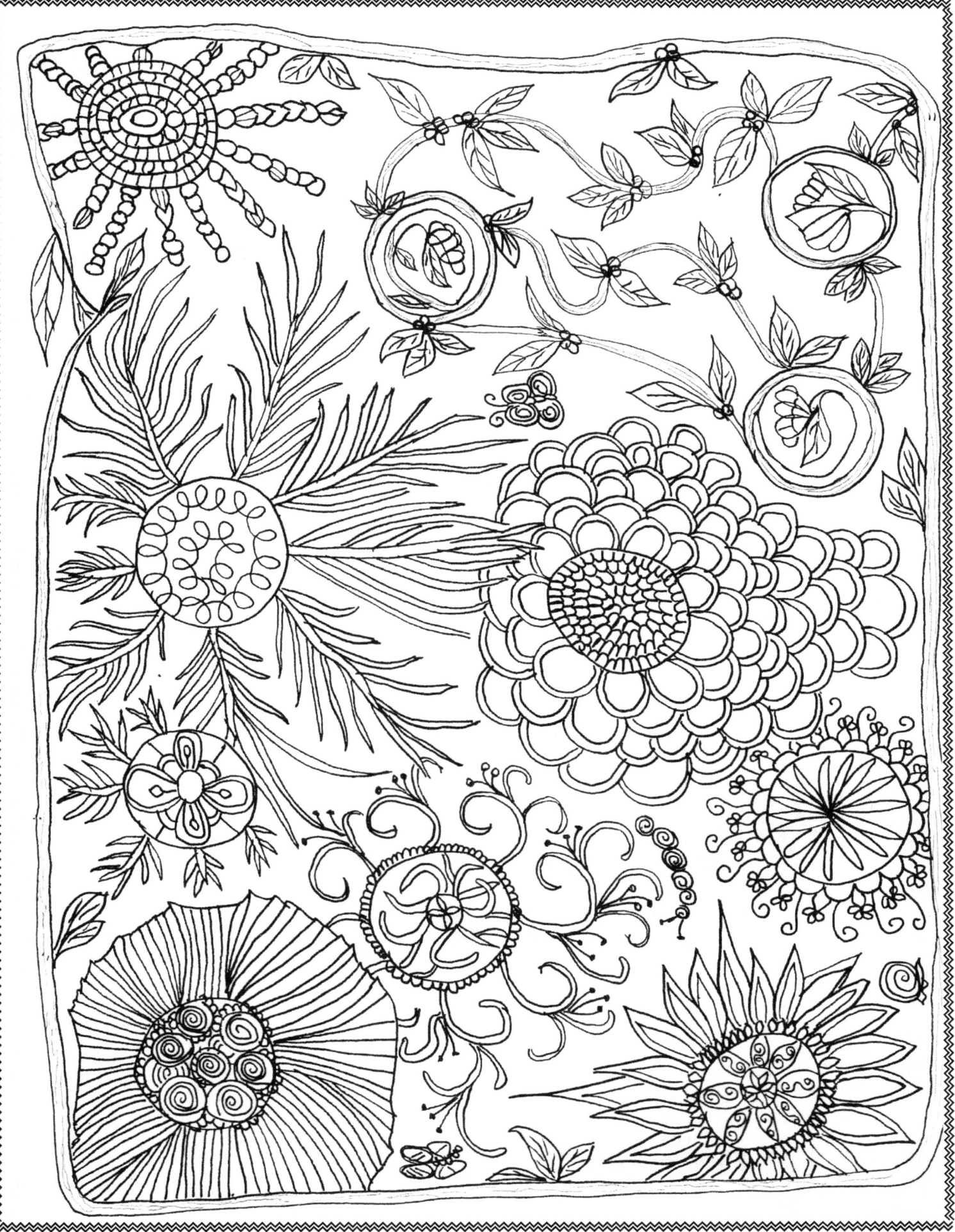

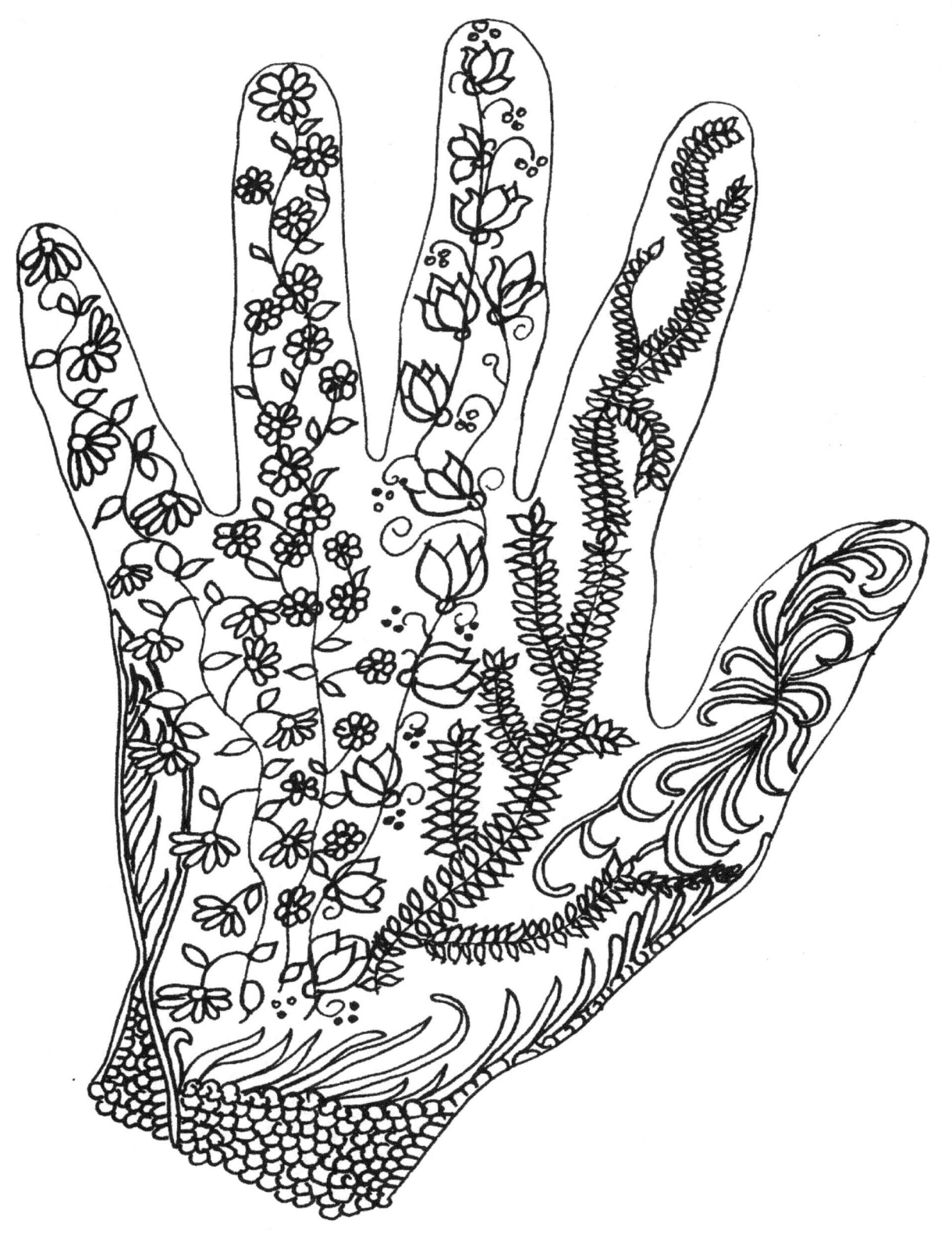

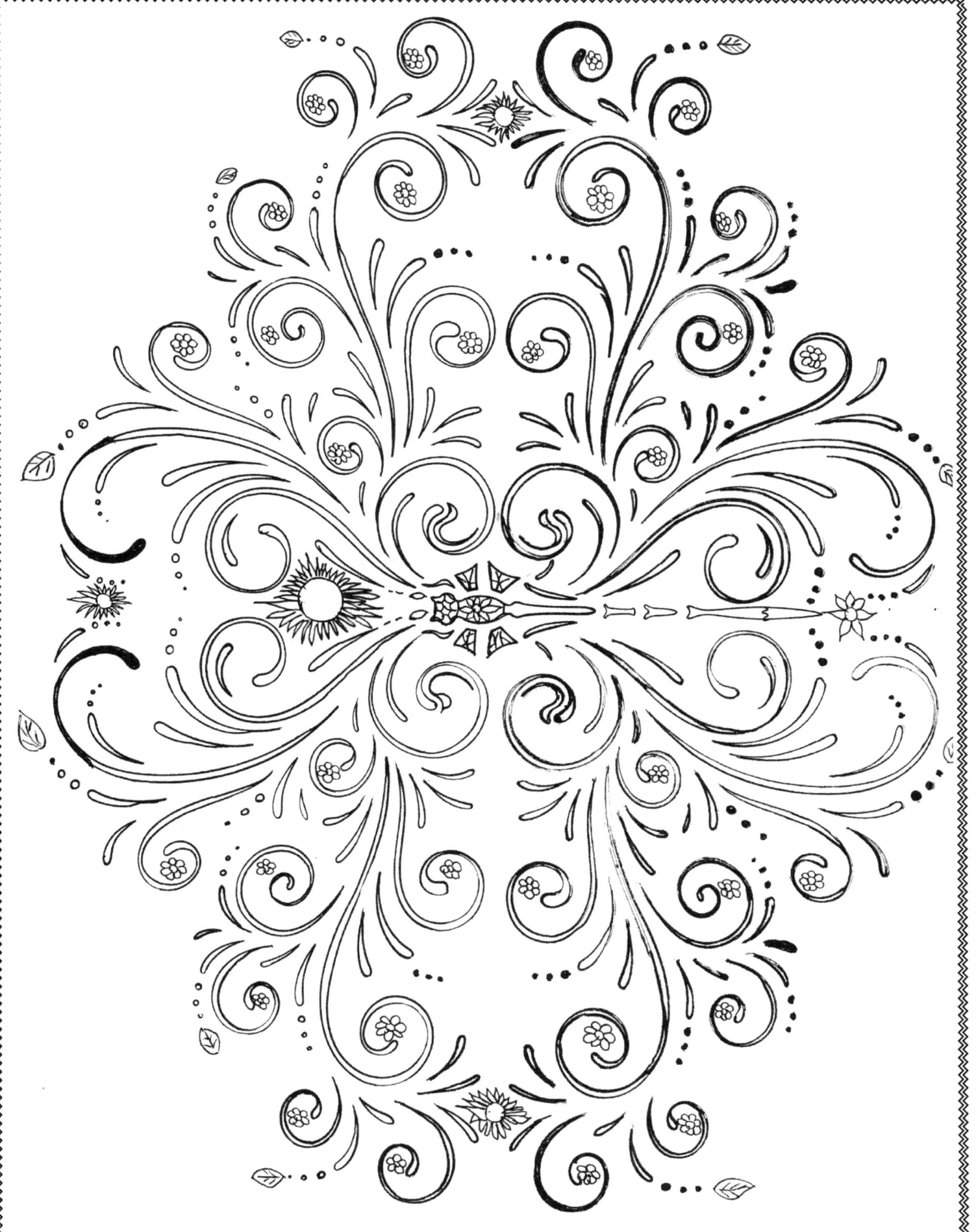

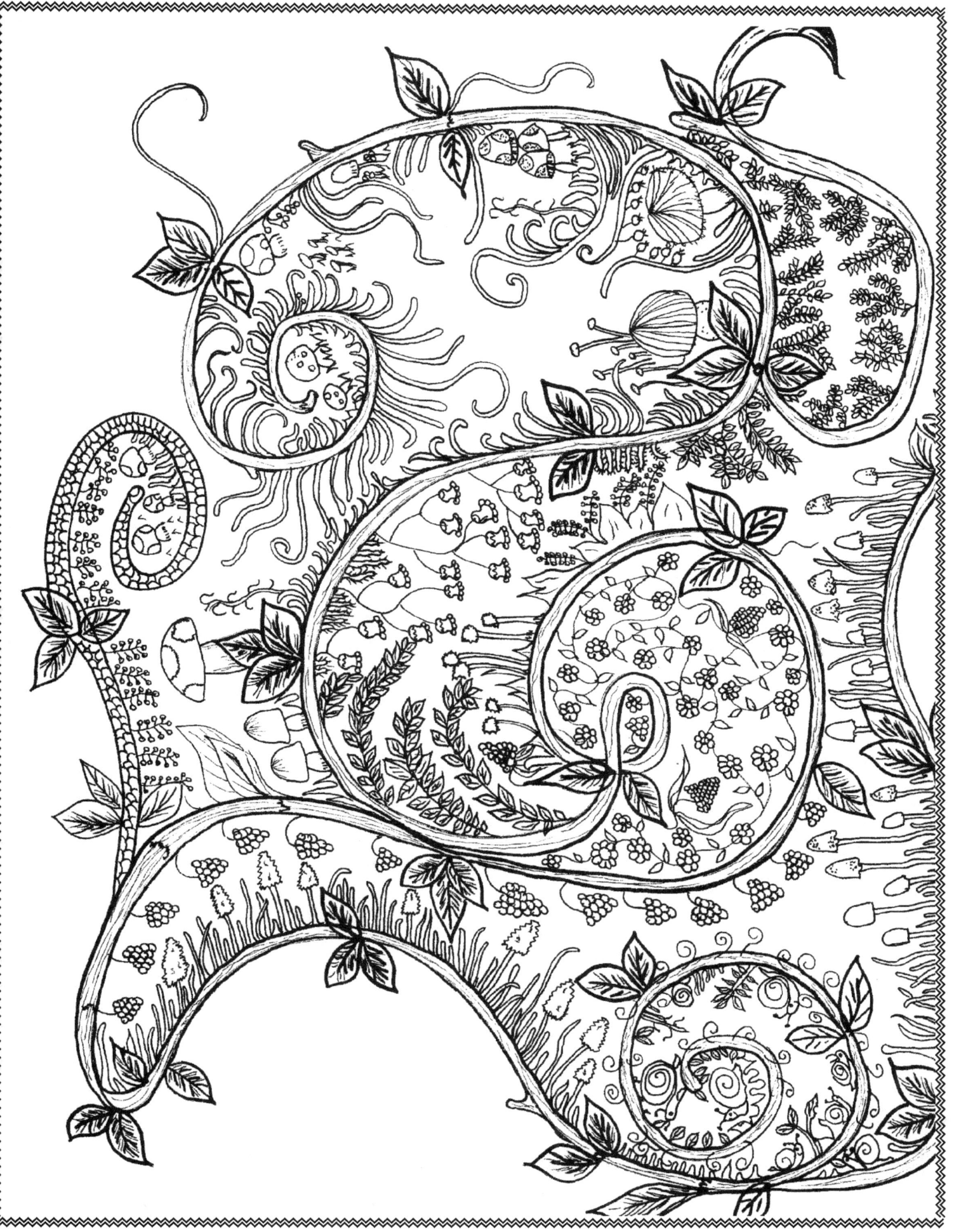

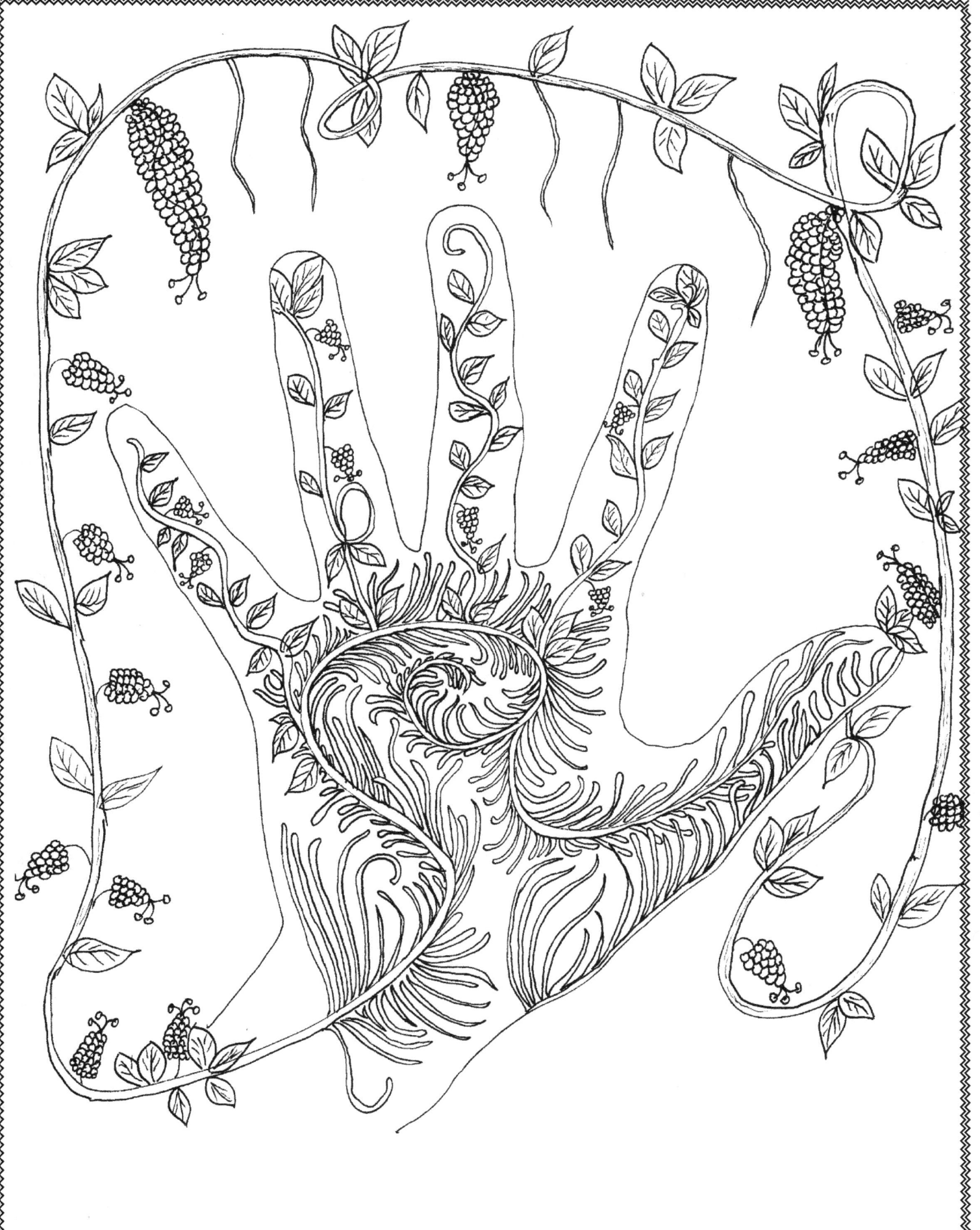

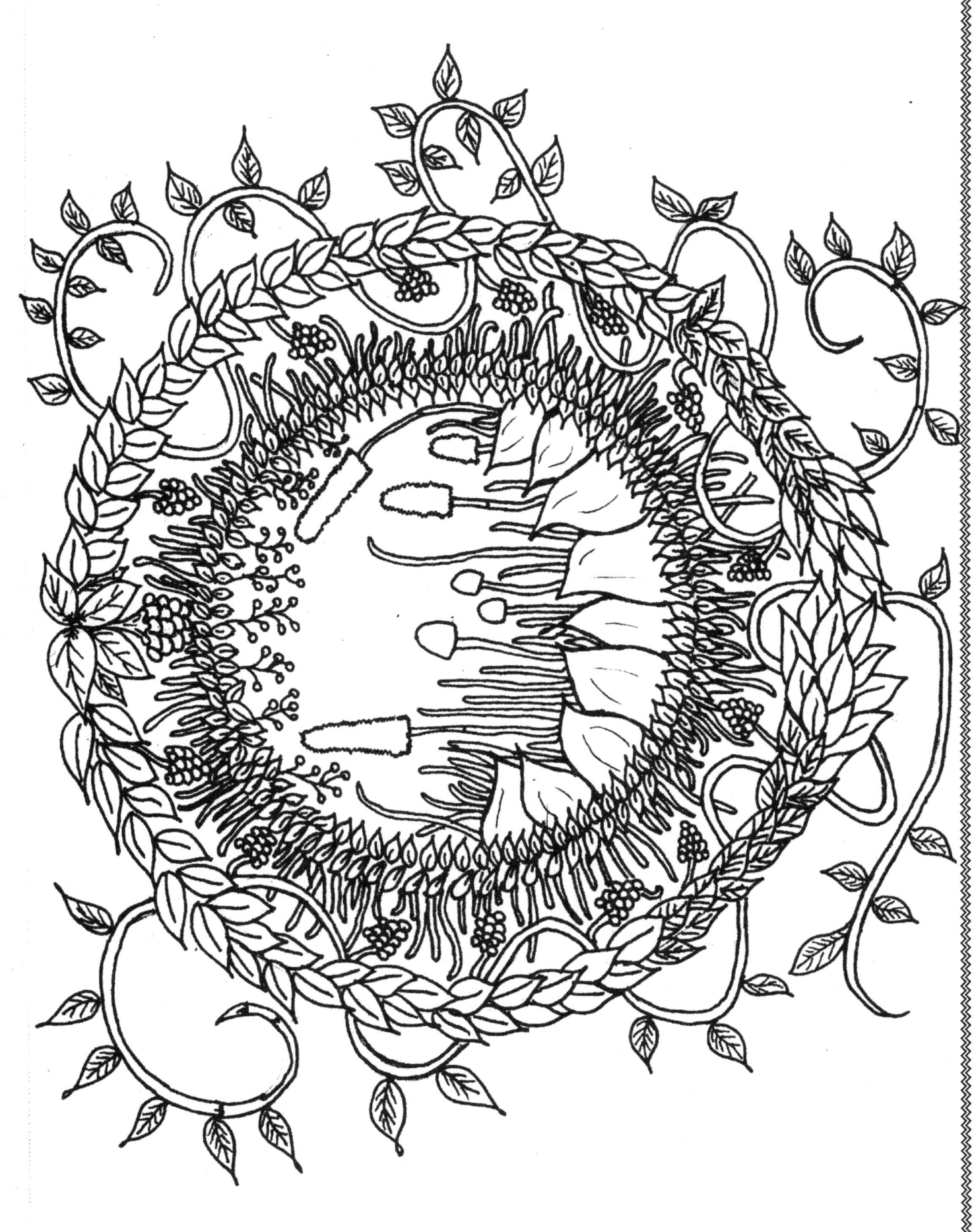

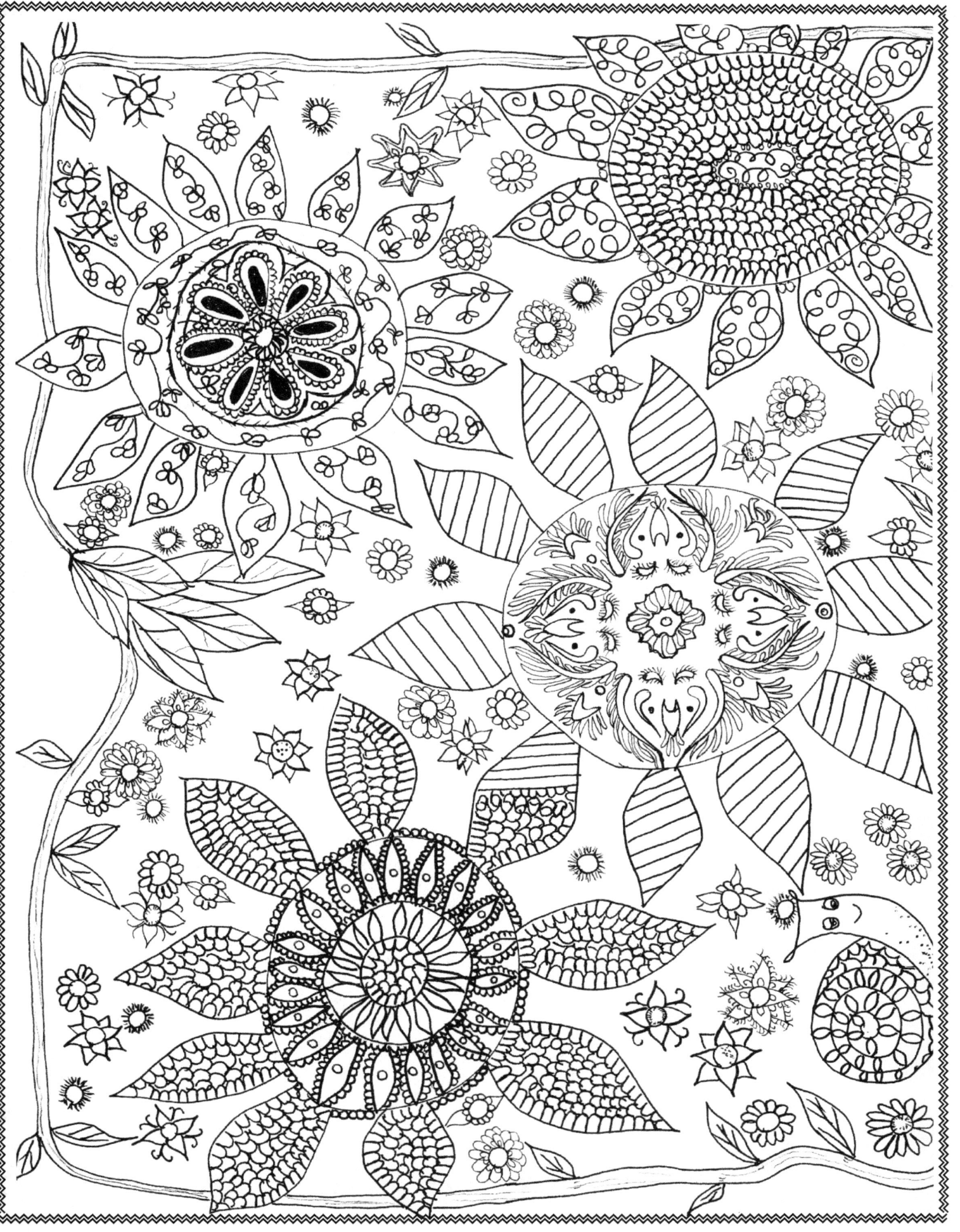

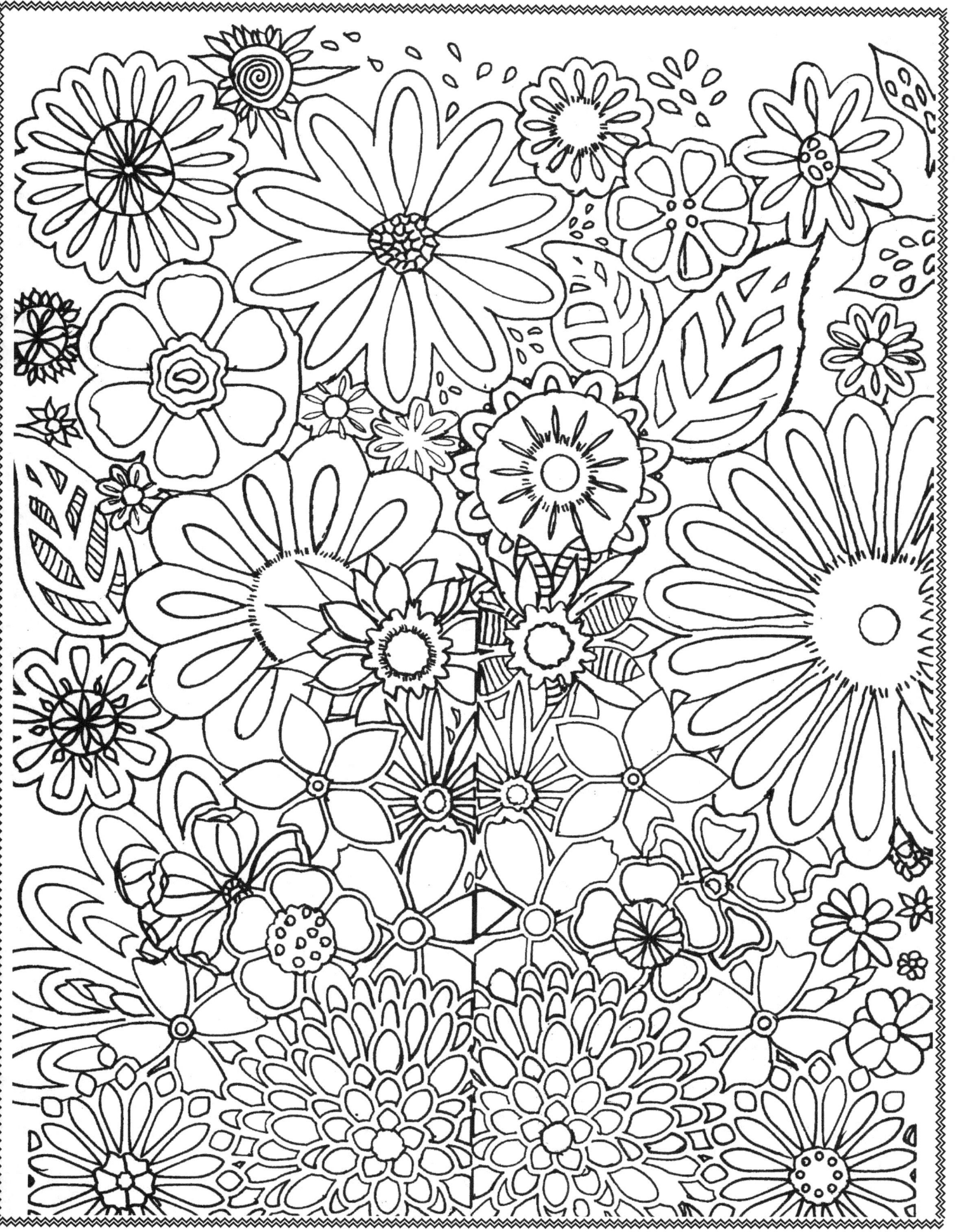

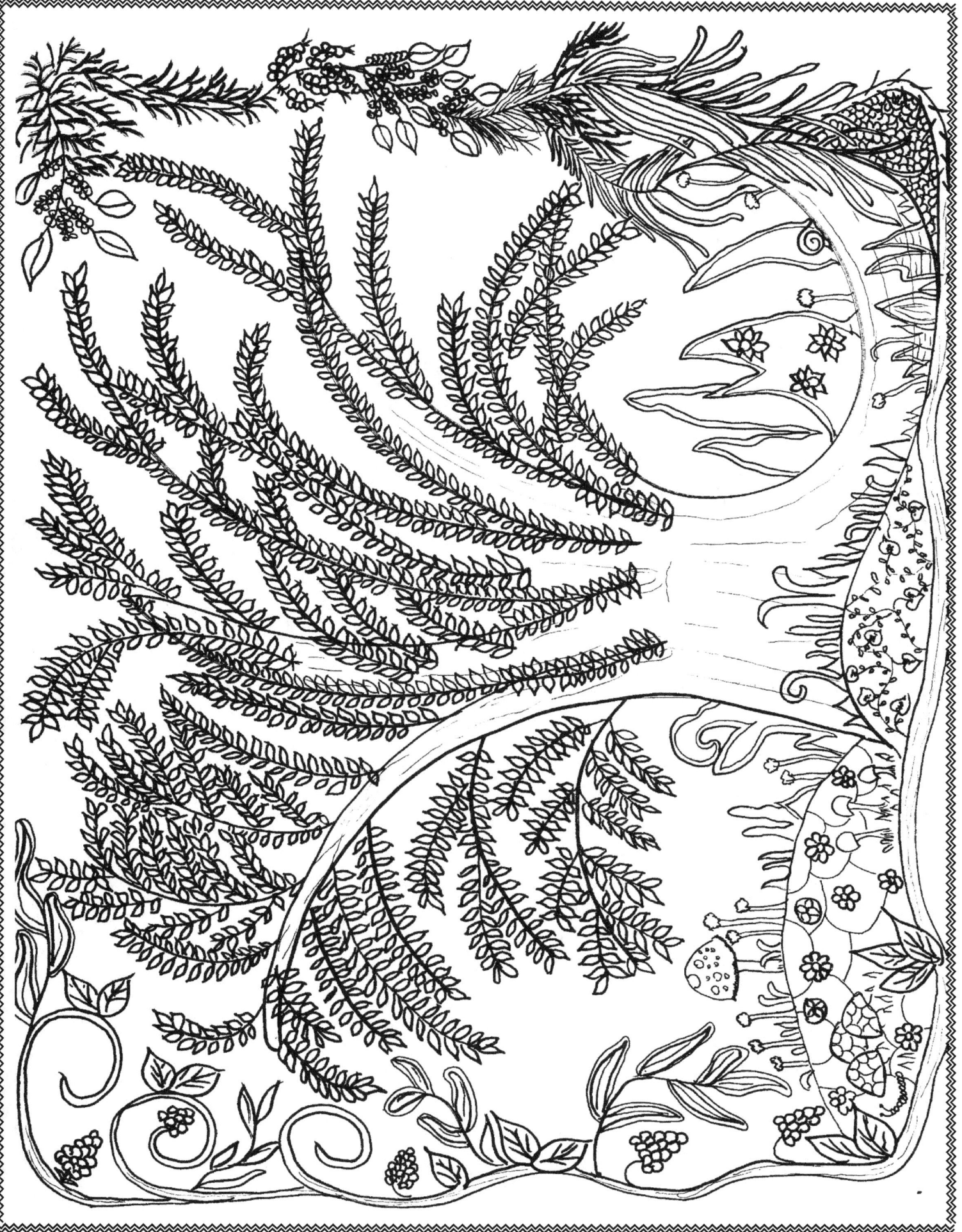

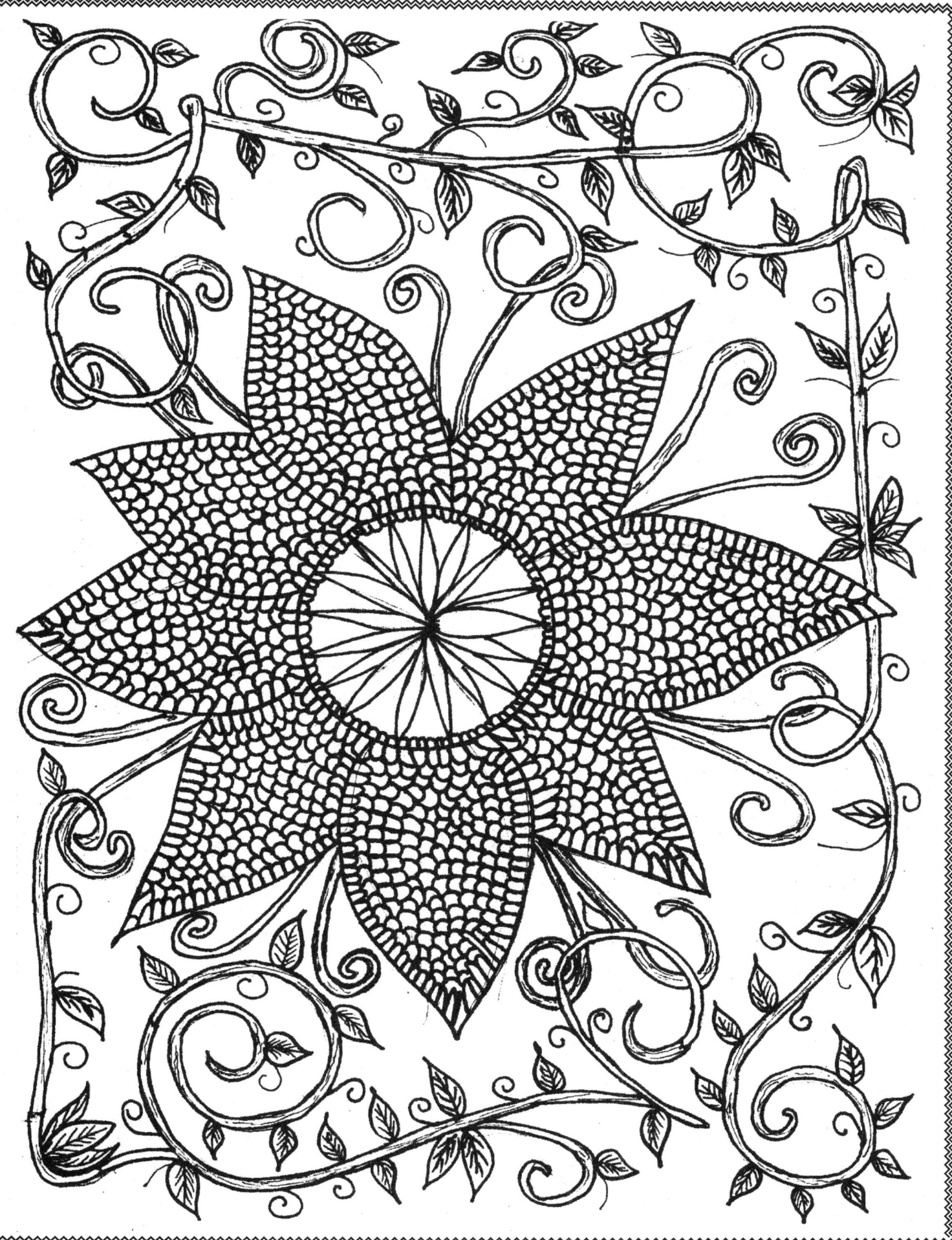

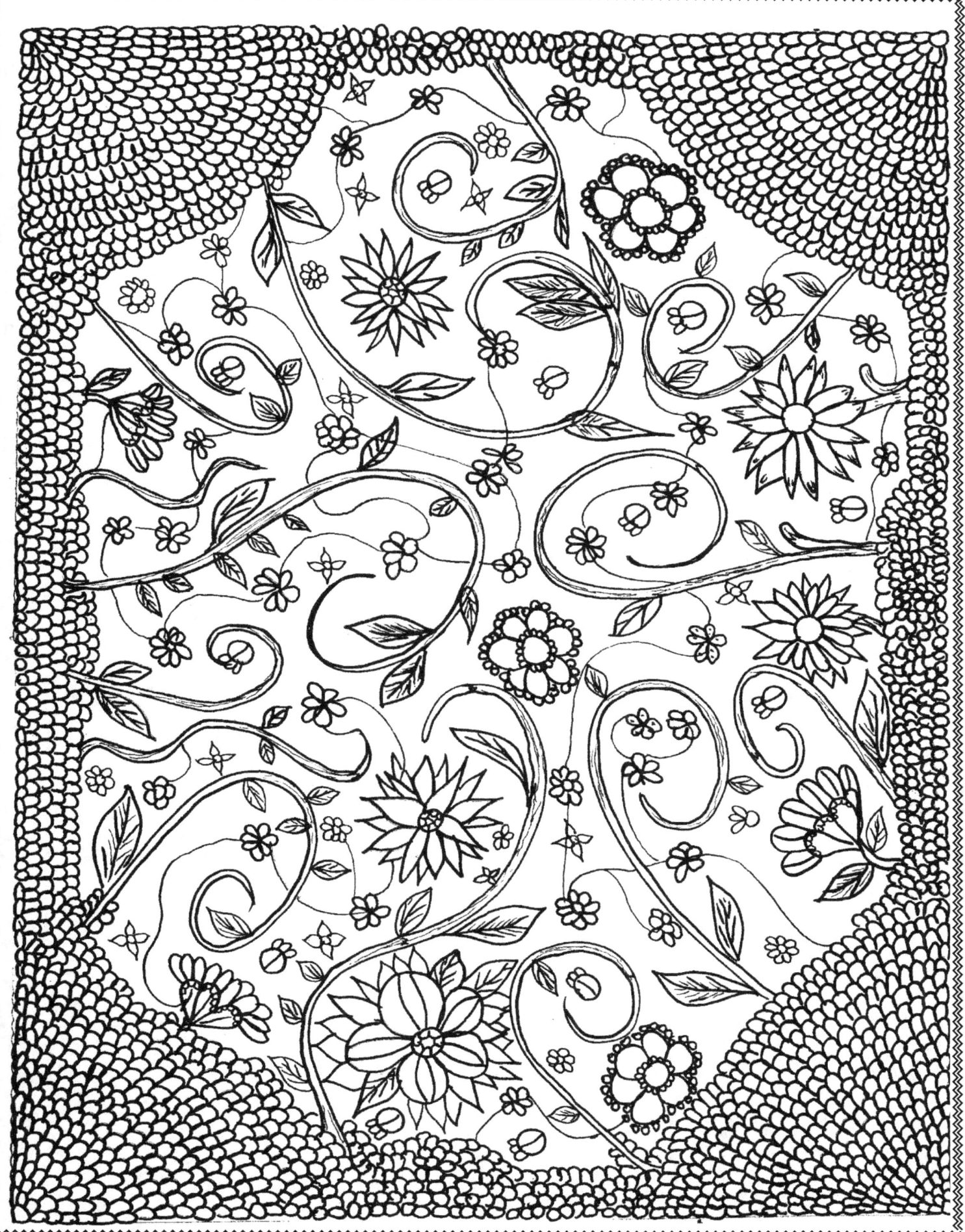

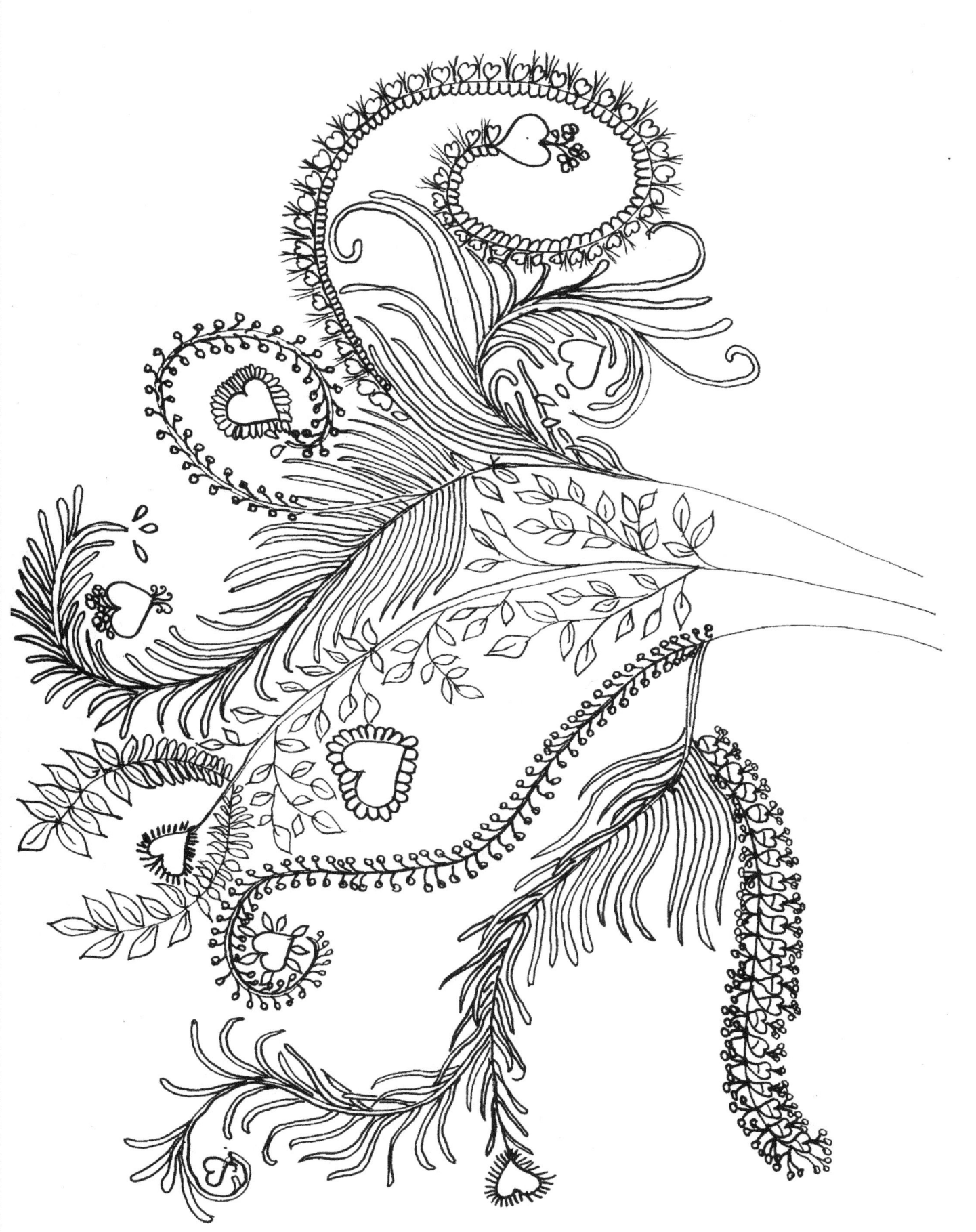

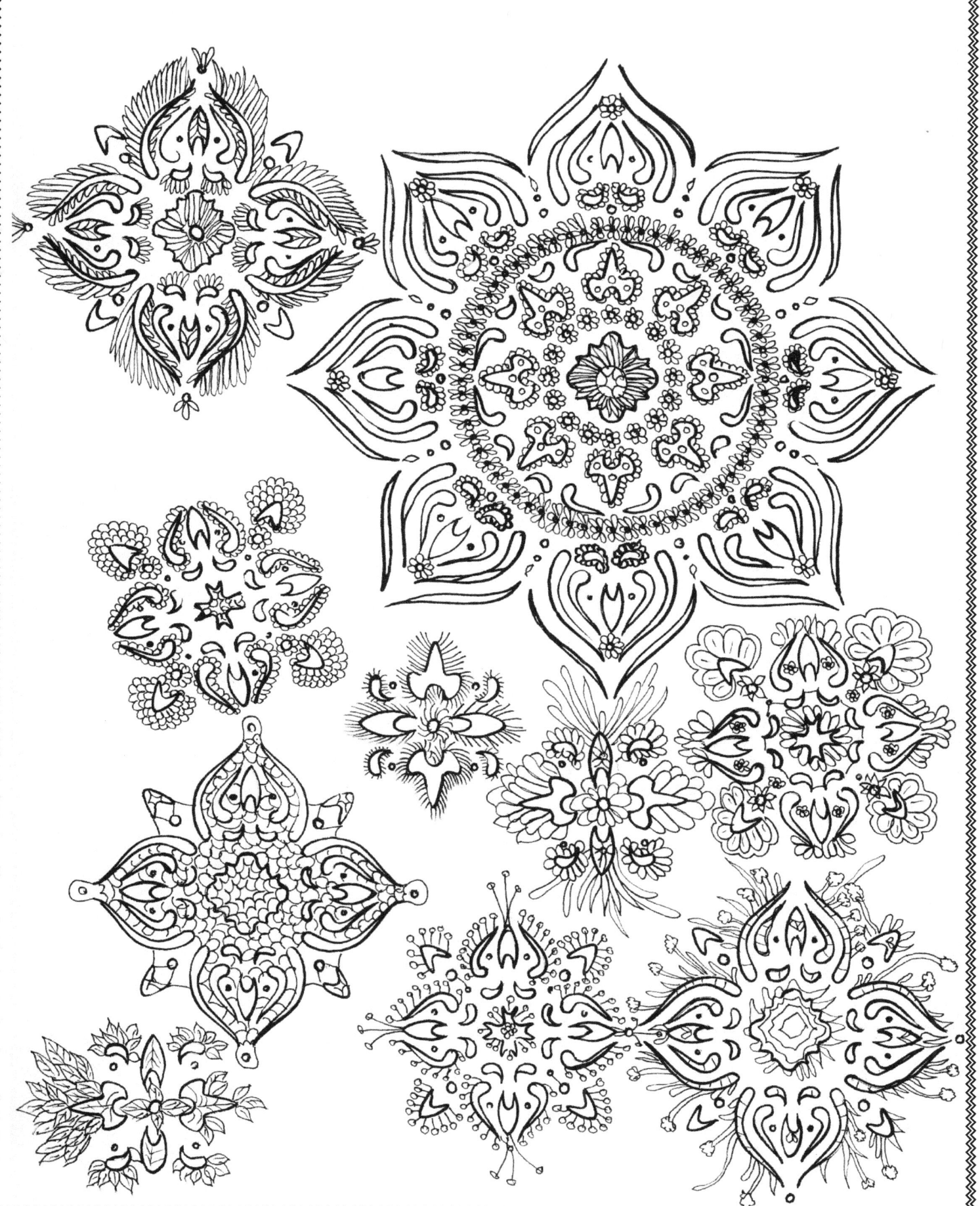

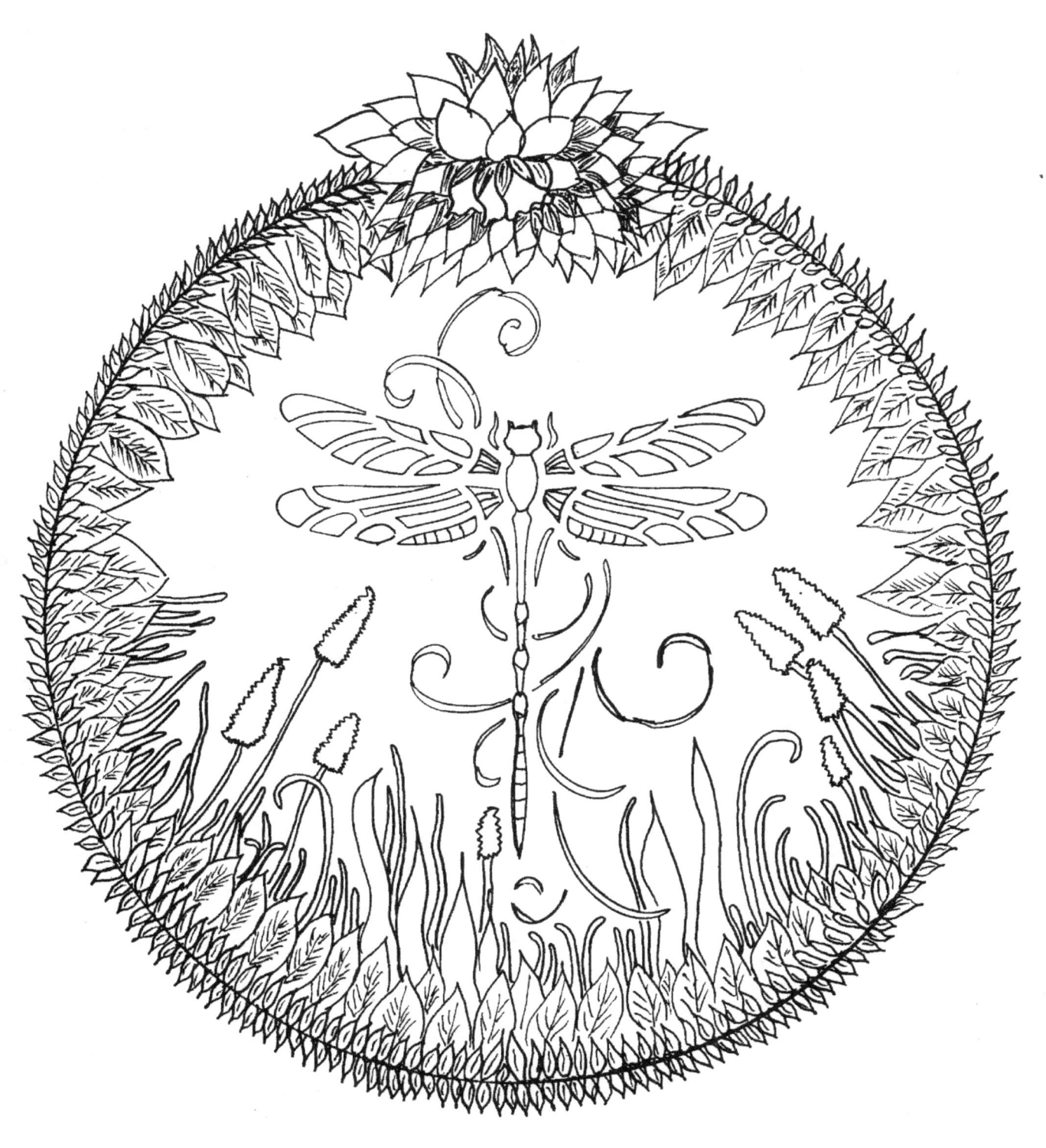

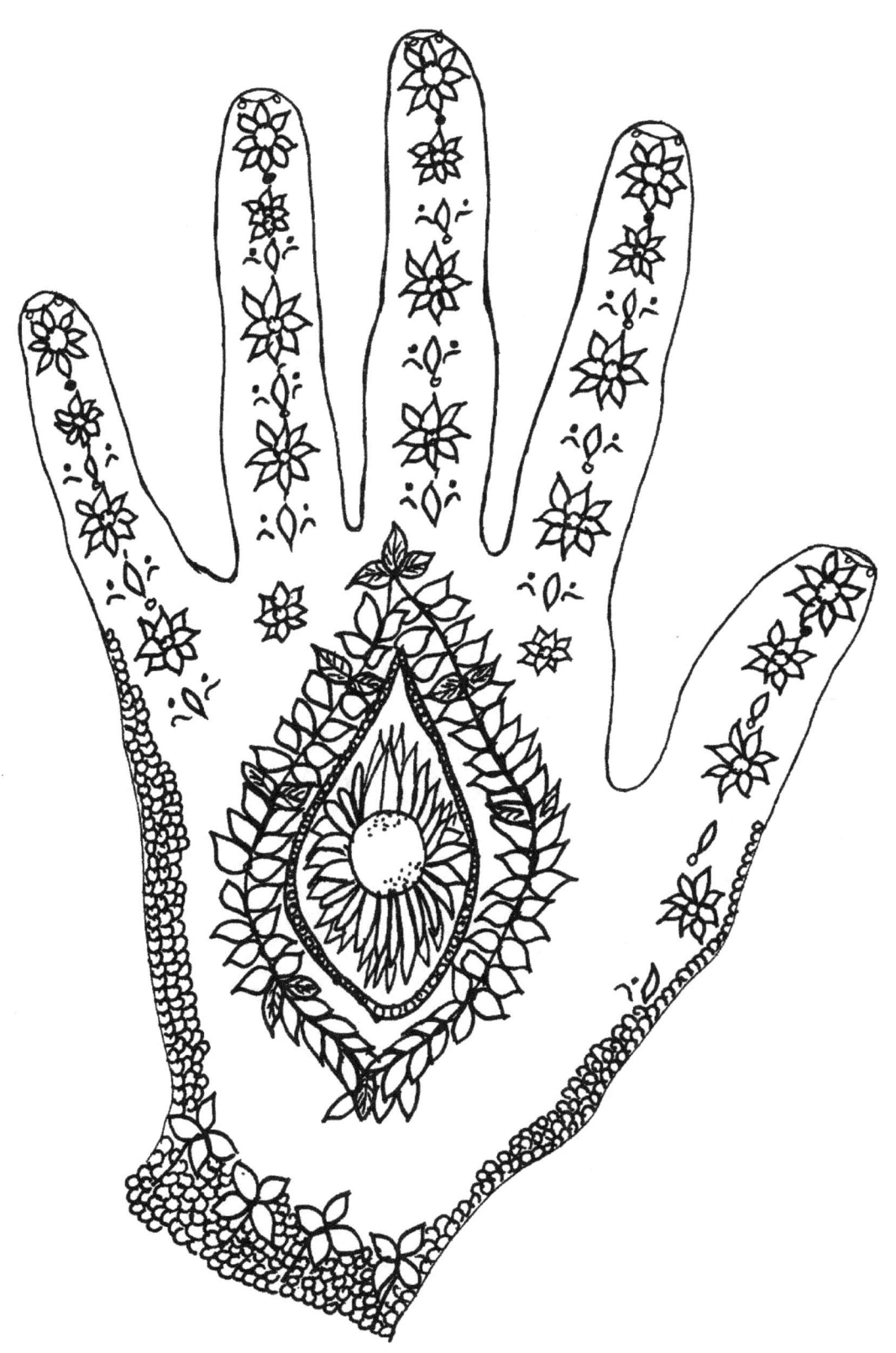

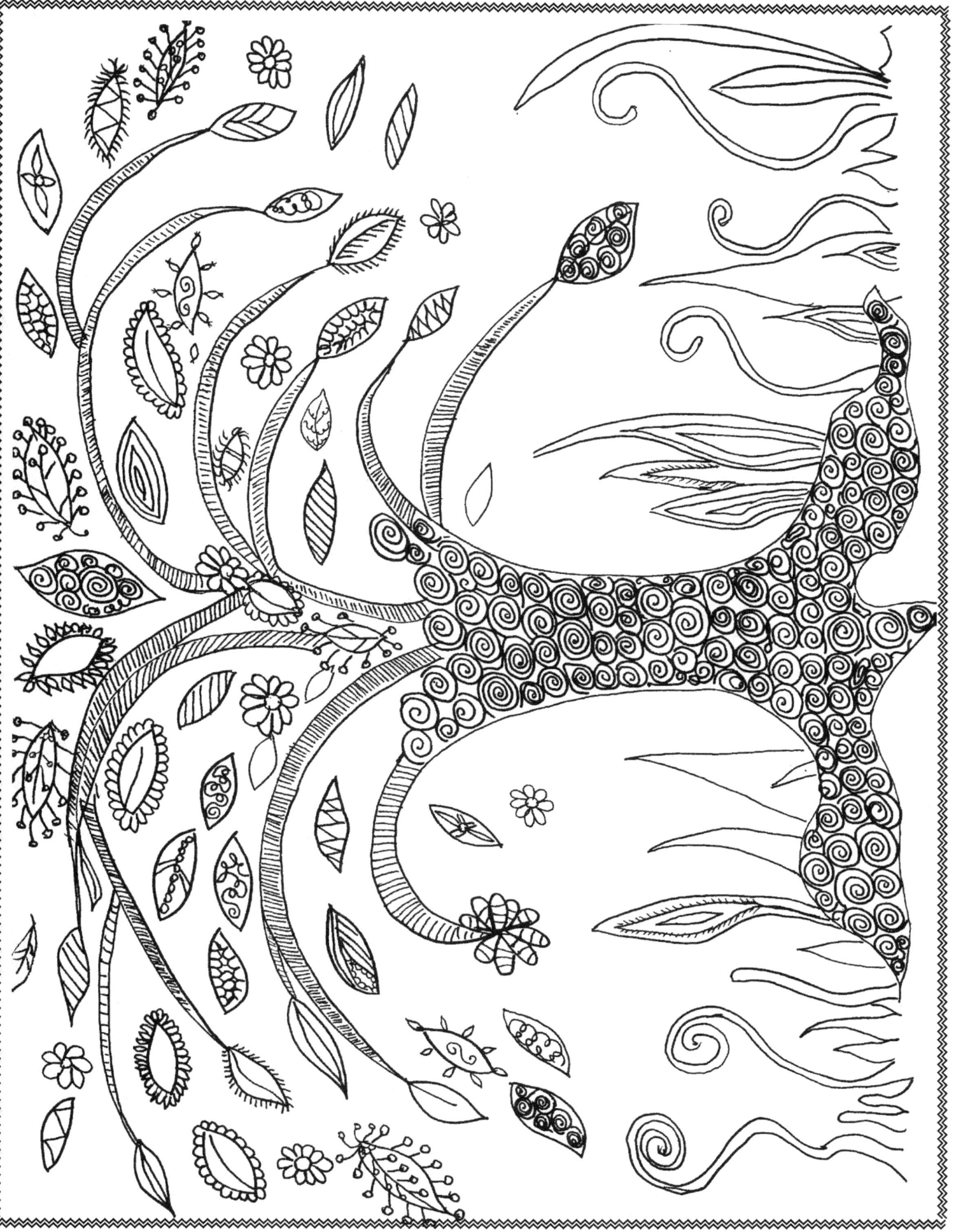

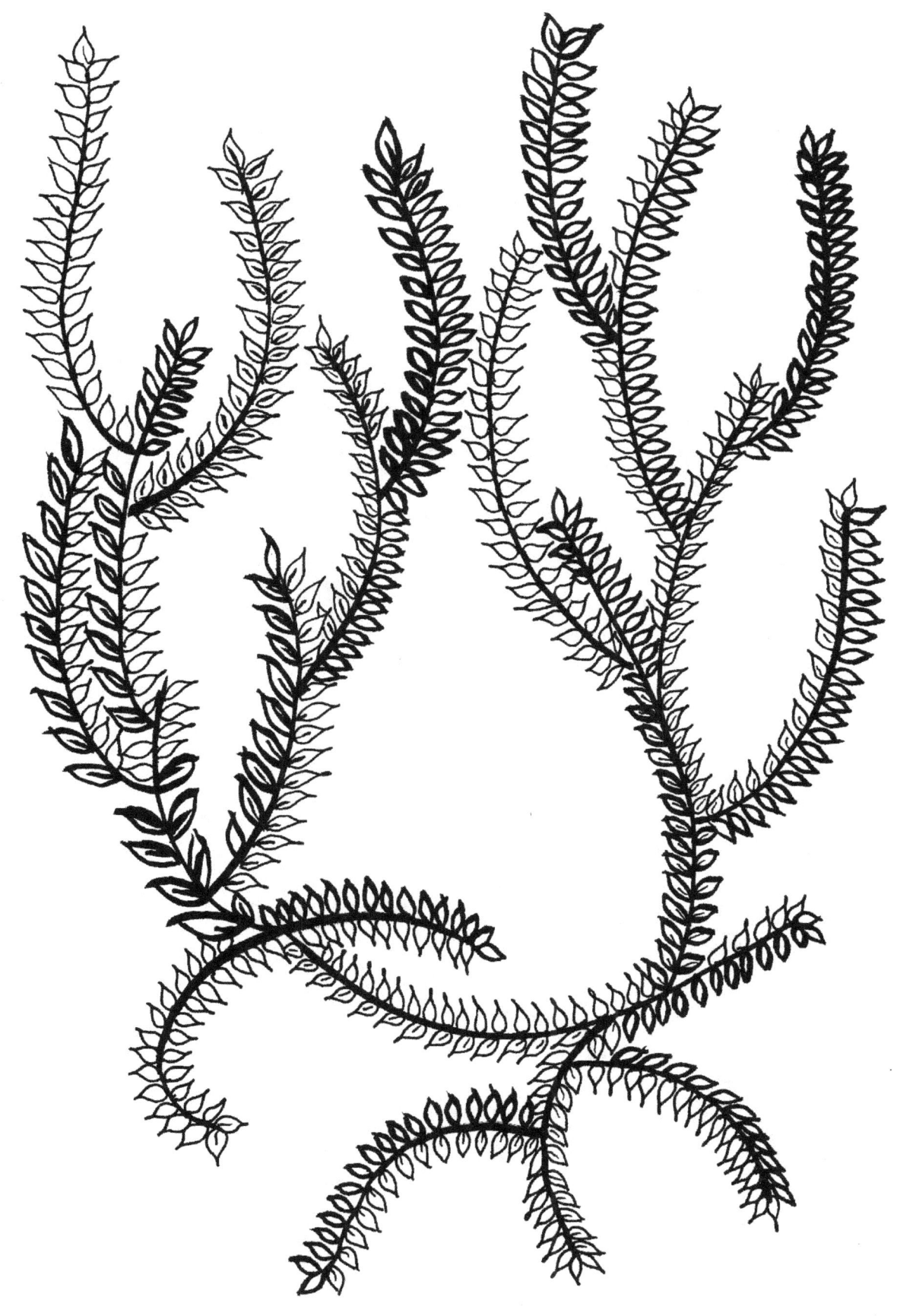

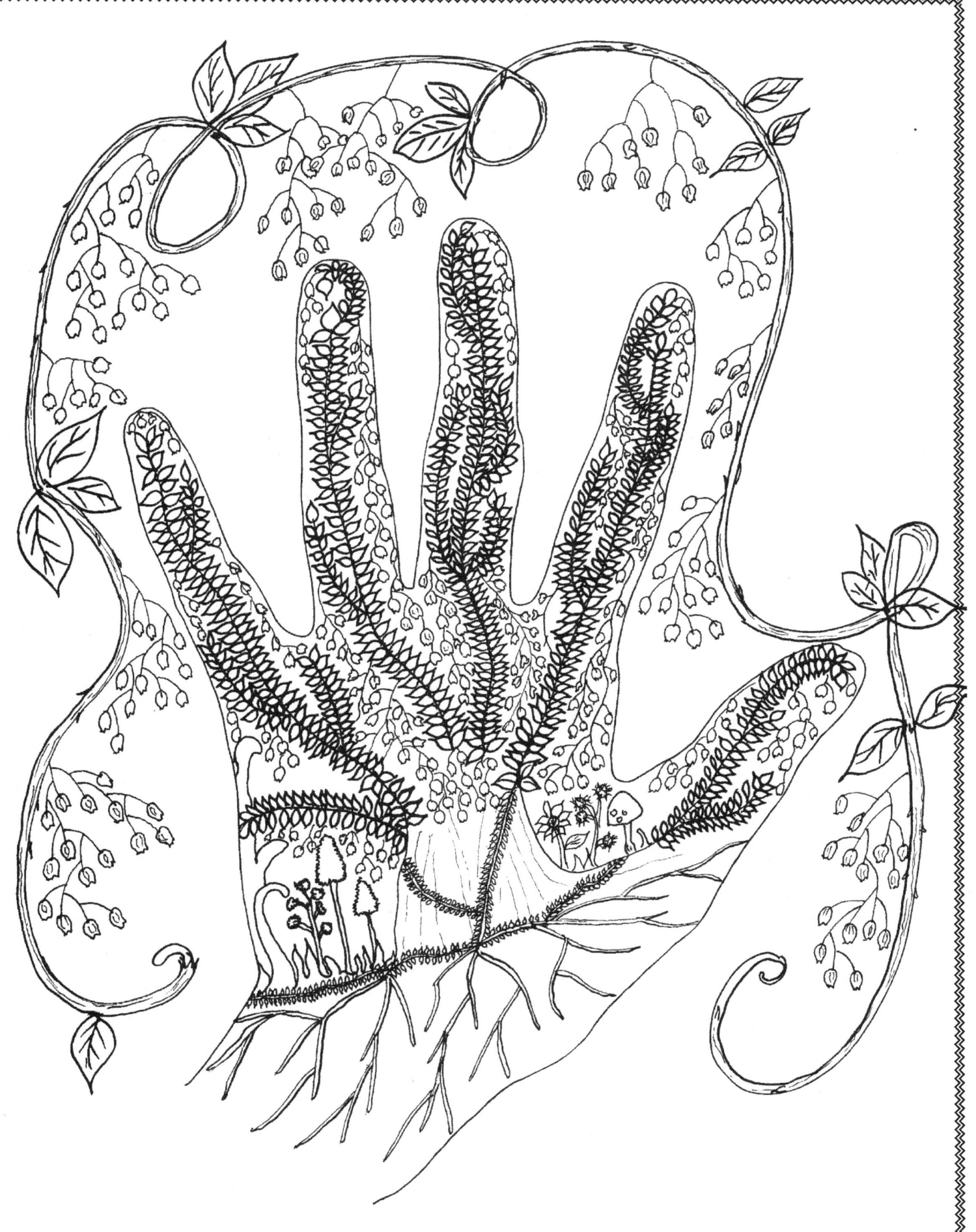

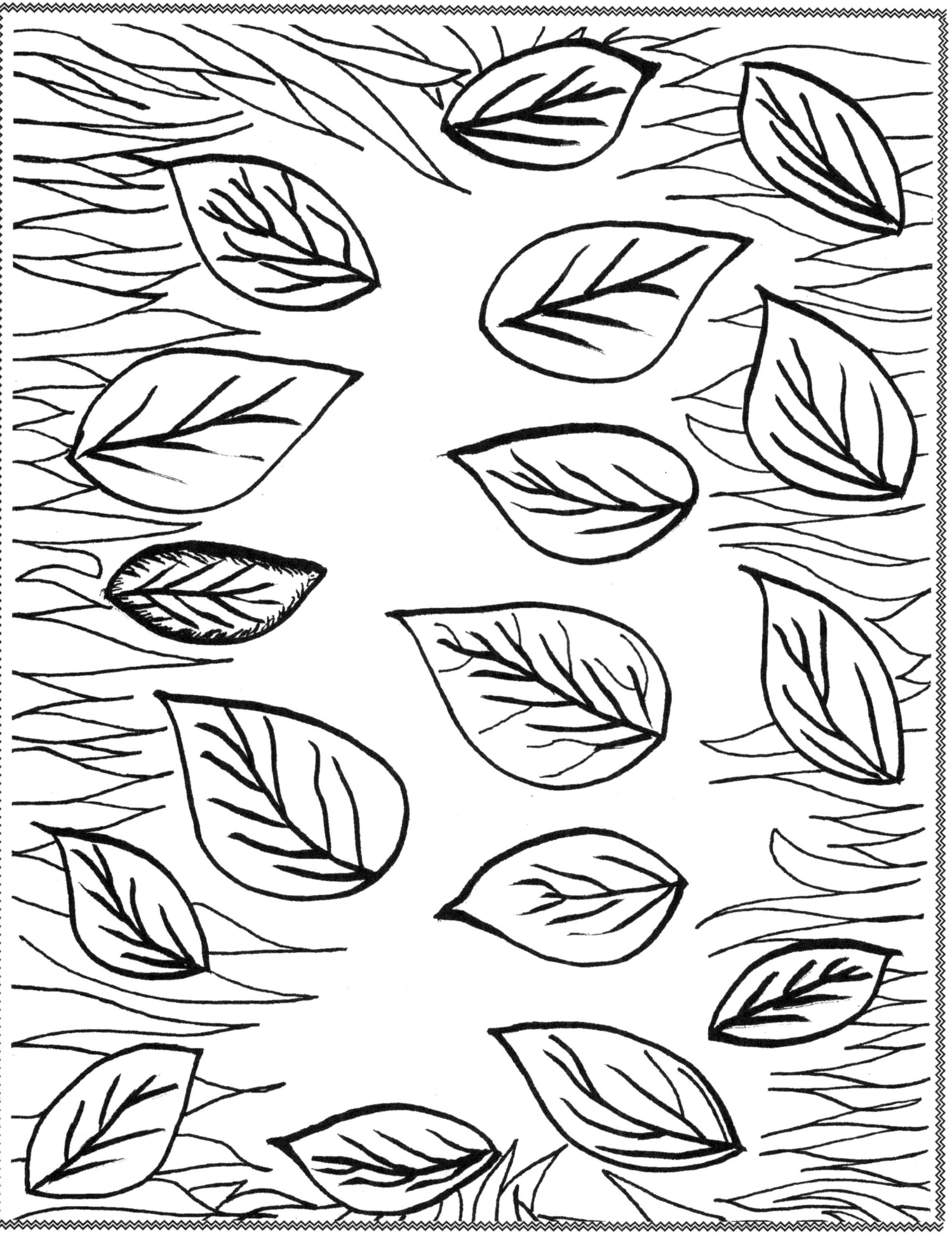

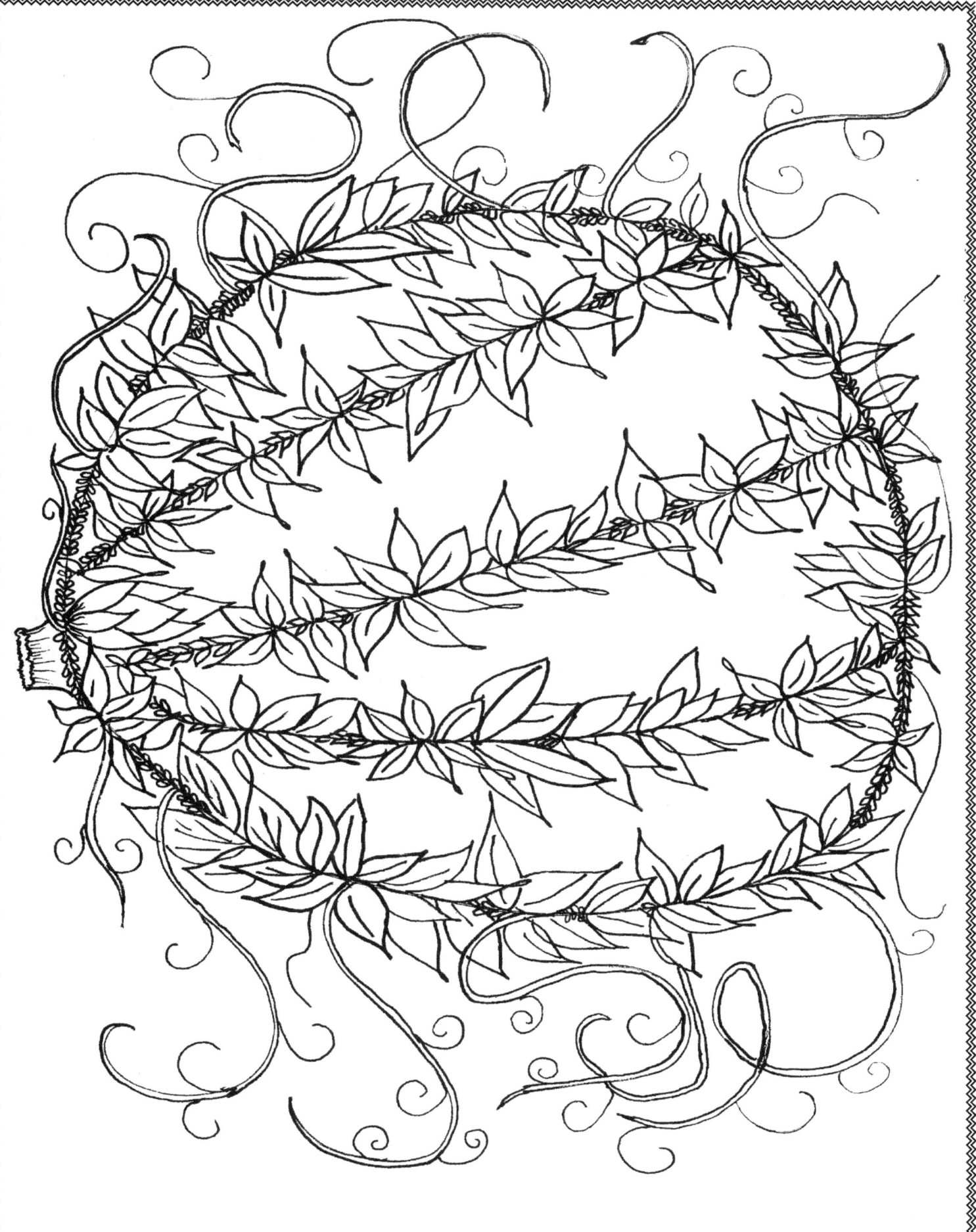

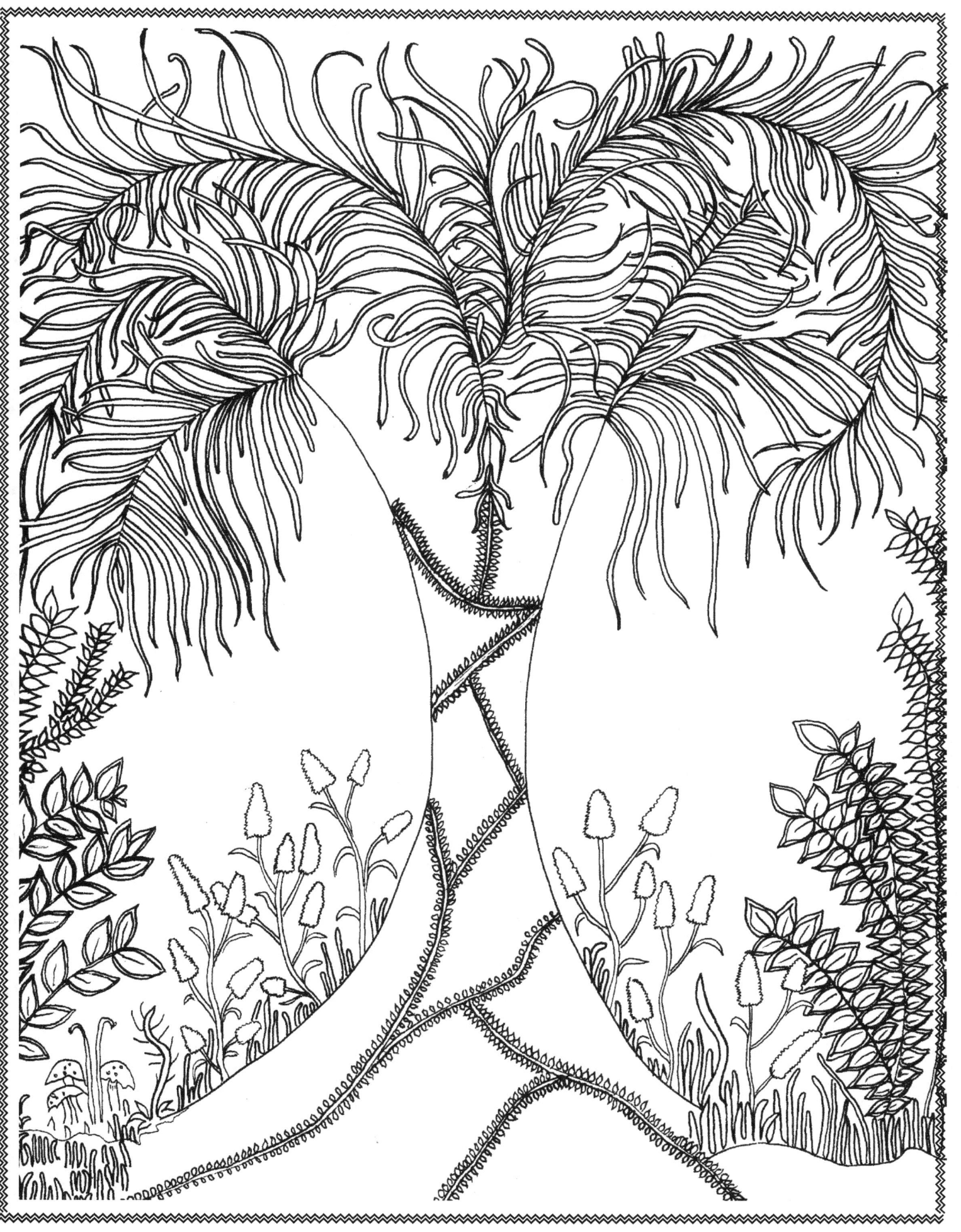

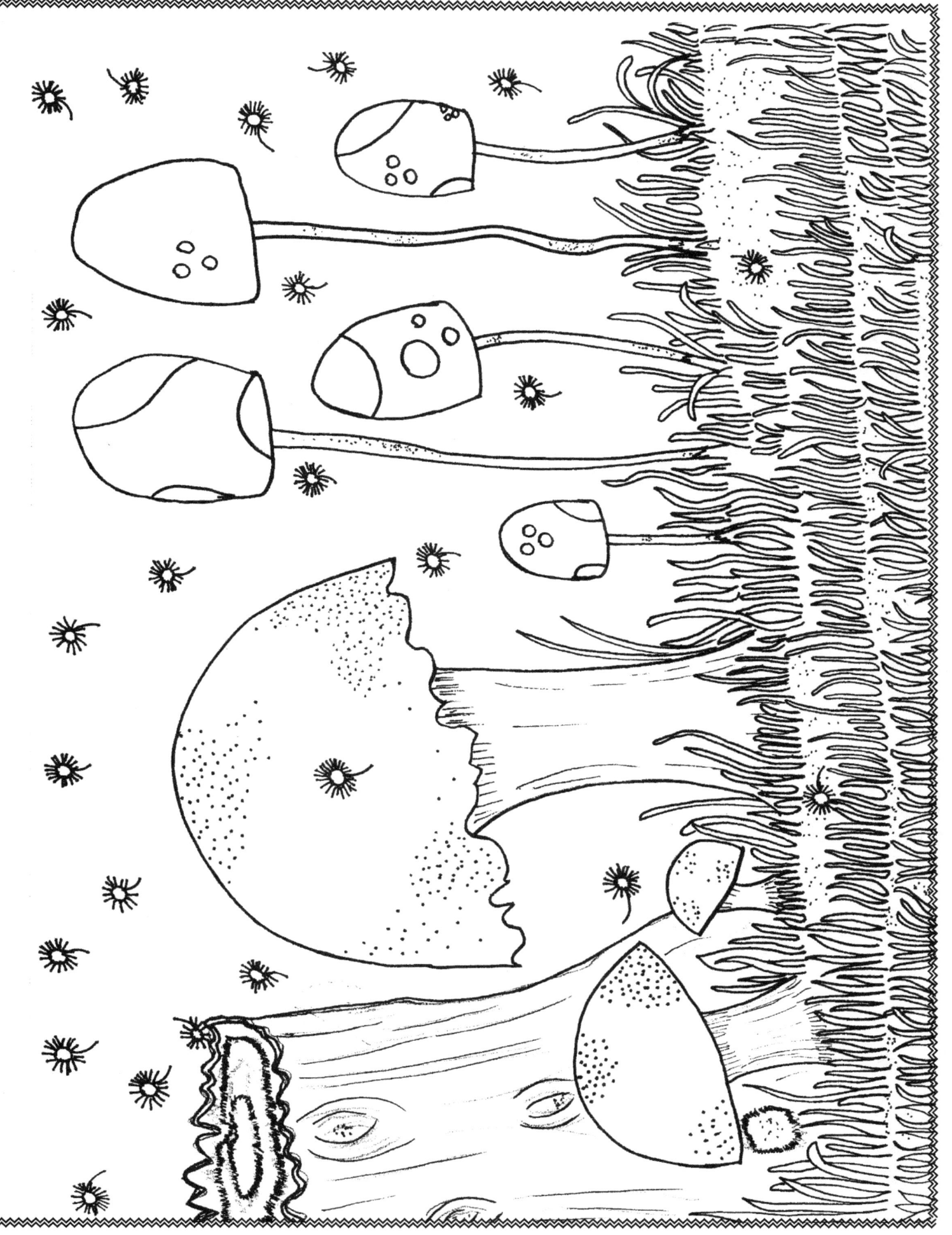

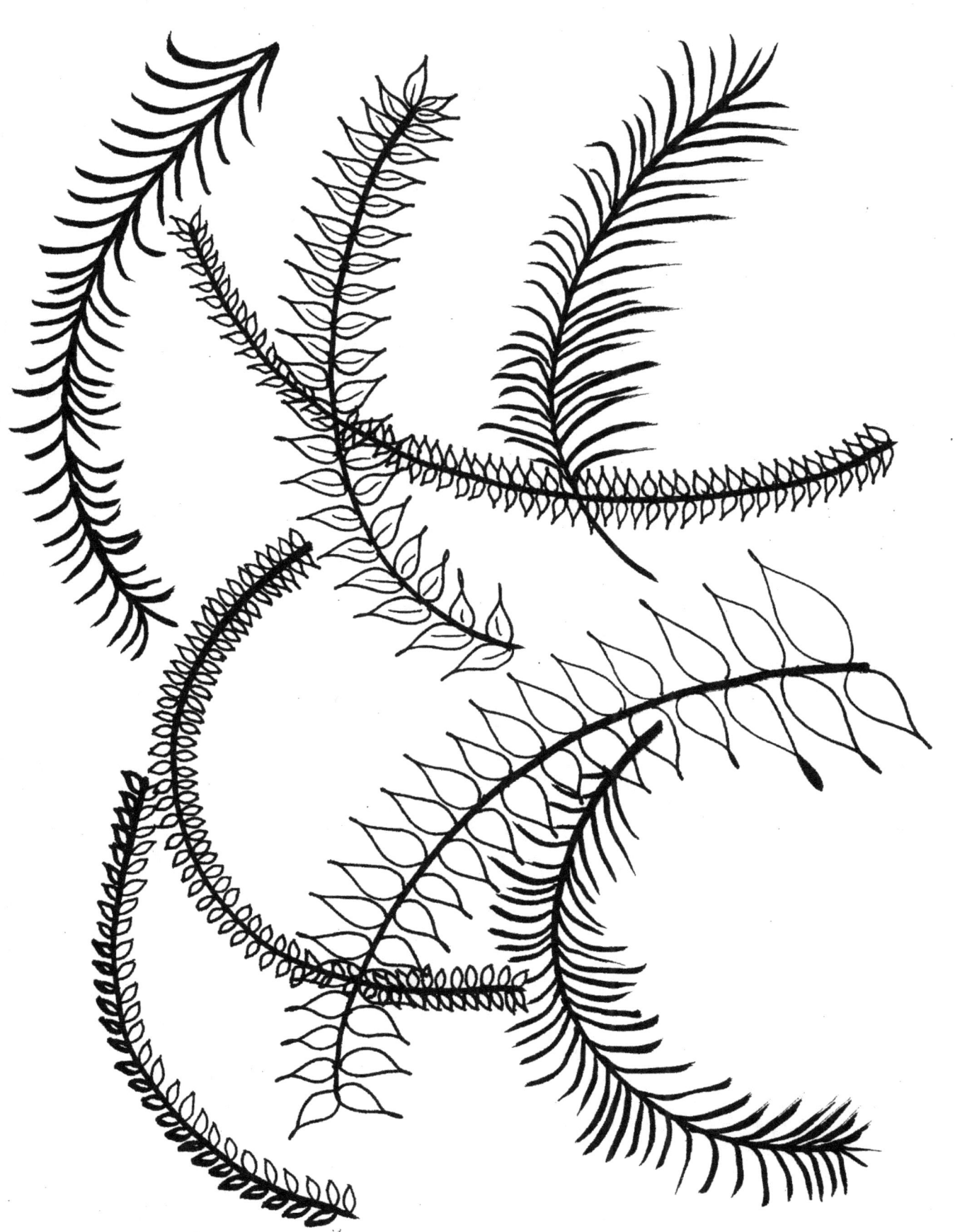

I hope you enjoyed this book!

Visit my Facebook page for upcoming projects

Thank You!

Sincerely,

Lei Faircloth

www.ingramcontent.com/pod-product-compliance
Lightning Source LLC
Chambersburg PA
CBHW062200220526
45470CB00009B/2884